THE WORLD IN A GRID
Latitude and Longitude

World Geography Book Grade 4 | Children's Geography & Cultures Books

BABY PROFESSOR
EDUCATION KIDS

First Edition, 2020

Published in the United States by Speedy Publishing LLC, 40 E Main Street, Newark, Delaware 19711 USA.

© 2020 Baby Professor Books, an imprint of Speedy Publishing LLC

All images in this book have been reproduced with the knowledge and prior consent of the artists concerned, and no responsibility is accepted by producer, publisher, or printer for any infringement of copyright or otherwise arising from the contents of this publication.

Baby Professor Books are available at special discounts when purchased in bulk for industrial and sales-promotional use. For details contact our Special Sales Team at Speedy Publishing LLC, 40 E Main Street, Newark, Delaware 19711 USA. Telephone (888) 248-4521 Fax: (210) 519-4043. www.speedybookstore.com

10 9 8 7 6 * 5 4 3 2 1

Print Edition: 9781541959804
Digital Edition: 9781541962804

See the world in pictures. Build your knowledge in style.
www.speedypublishing.com

TABLE OF CONTENTS

What is a grid and what does it have to do with the Earth? A grid is a group of parallel lines that are equally spaced between each other. Some lines are in a vertical position, up and down, while others are in a horizontal position or across, right to left. The vertical and horizontal lines crisscross to make up squares or rectangles. These lines are called section lines. By using the basic concepts of a grid, the Earth can be broken down into different areas. By using a geographic grid system, the exact location of any place on Earth can be determined. This book will explain why and how this happens.

A 3D image of planet Earth with its imaginary grids

MAPS AND GLOBES

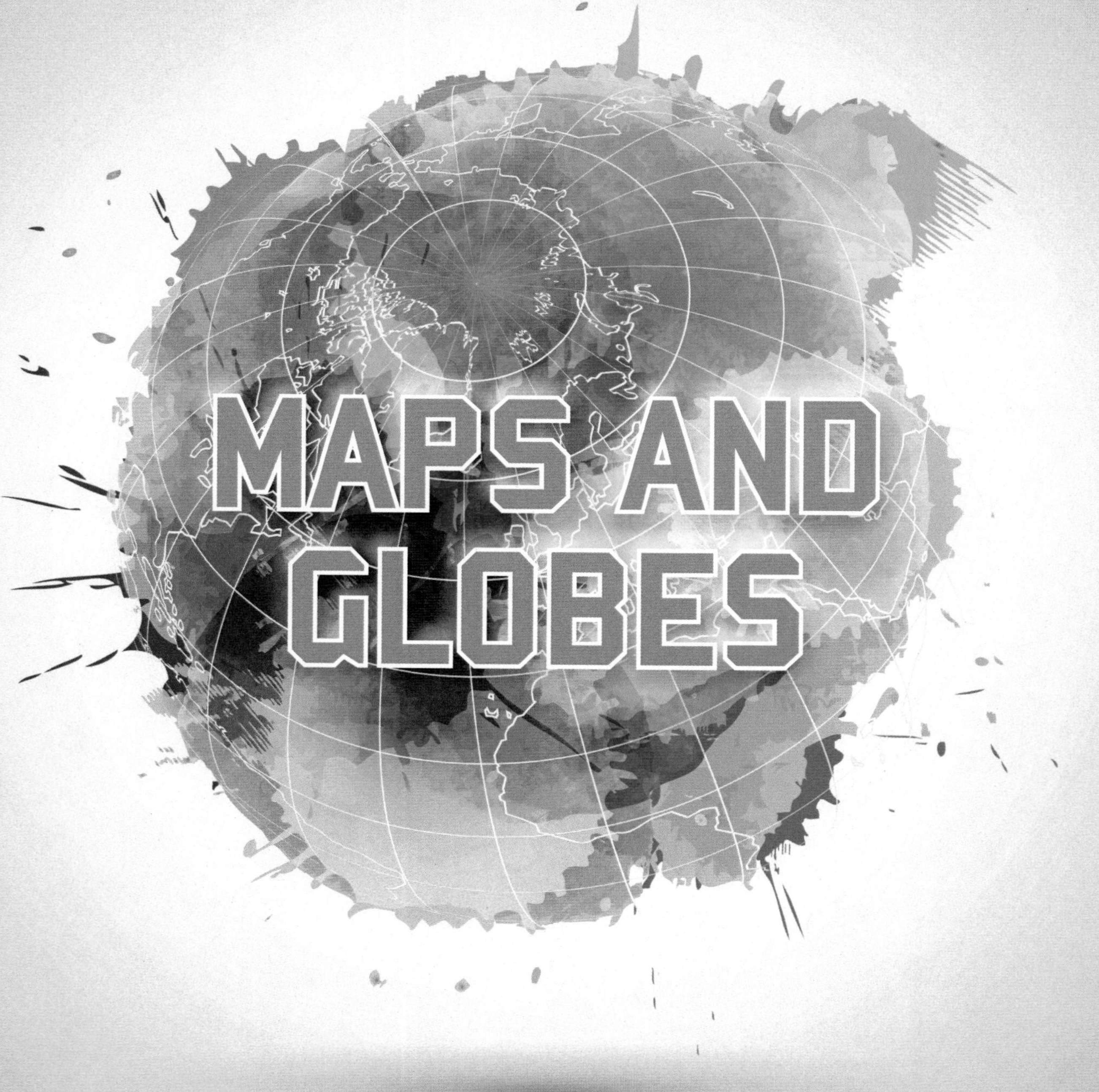

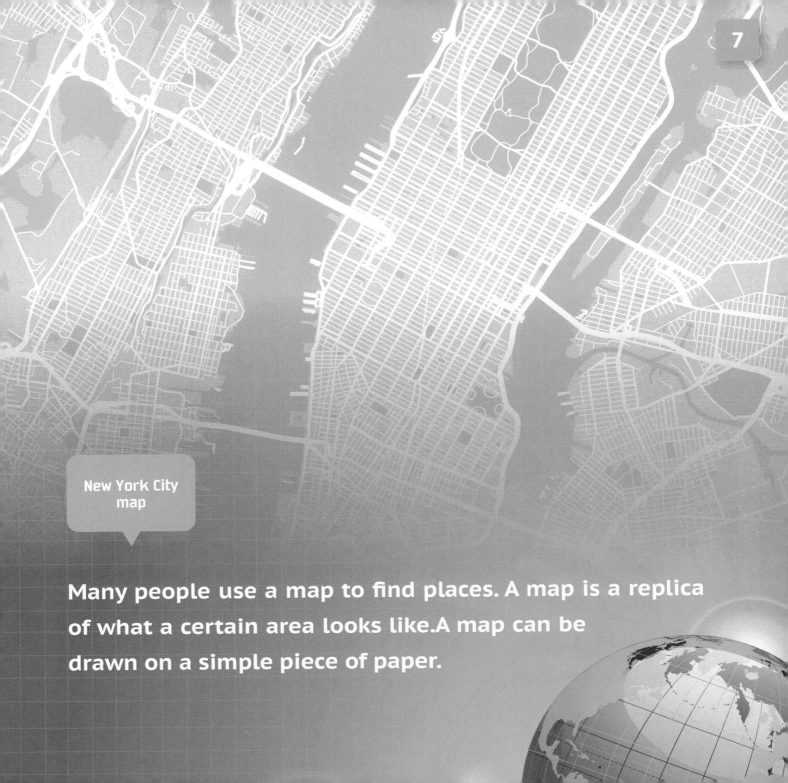

New York City
map

Many people use a map to find places. A map is a replica
of what a certain area looks like. A map can be
drawn on a simple piece of paper.

A map can be used to find short distances, such as from a person's home to the local supermarket or school.

An illustration of a city map route

A map that is bought in a convenience store, for example, may be of a local town or city. It will have a grid system to show the different streets and it may have an index to show where different landmarks are situated. However, it is still on a flat piece of paper.

Tourists looking on a City map

A globe, which is round and resembles the shape of the Earth, gives a visual perception of where the different countries and oceans are located on Earth. A globe is a great source of putting things into perspective in the way that a map cannot.

A globe gives a visual perception of where countries and oceans are located on Earth.

For example, if your family were planning a trip from your home in the United States to Sydney, Australia, a globe would be a great way to measure the distance between these two points.

A child looking at a globe

You could easily put one finger on one place and another finger on the other place. You would notice the distance as it appears on the Earth because a globe is of a similar shape.

You can use your fingers to trace the distance between one state to another on the globe.

Children measure distance on world map

However, while a map or a globe are useful, pinpointing every little place on Earth with accuracy requires certain criteria. For this, we need a special system and this system uses what is known as lines of latitude and longitude.

LINES OF LATITUDE AND LONGITUDE

Lines of Latitude   Lines of Longitude

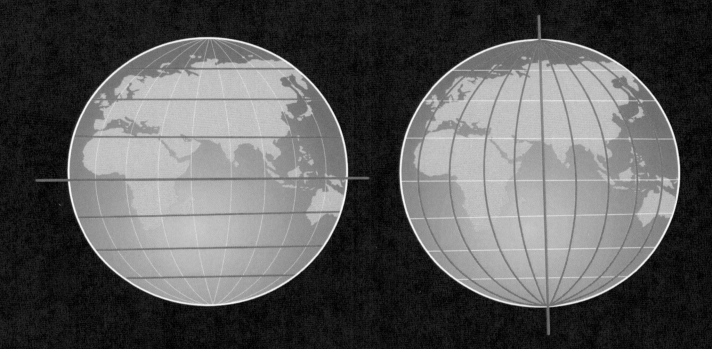

Lines of latitude and longitude are the names that are given to the imaginary lines that go around the Earth. They run in different directions and in so doing form a grid. They are used to show where different things are located on Earth.

LINES OF LATITUDE

Lines of latitude form a circular pattern around the Earth from east to west. They run parallel to each other. To run parallel means that they run side by side, but they never meet. In fact, each line in the lines of latitude have an equal space between them.

Latitude form a circular pattern around the Earth from east to west

LATITUDE

The Equator, which is the center of the Earth and where the Earth is at its thickest point, is considered the middle or center line of the lines of latitude. Due to the Equator running parallel with these lines, parallels or parallels of latitude can be used as other terms to describe the lines of latitude.

The Equator is the middle or center line of the lines of latitude.

Equator line

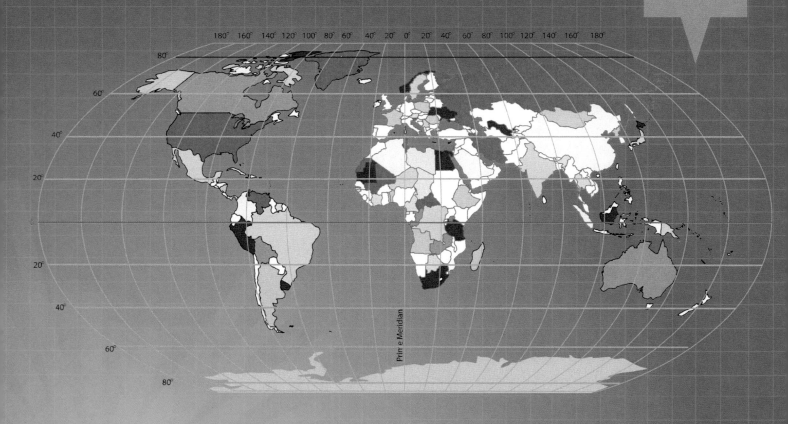

Equator is line zero in latitude

Because the Equator is the centre line, it is the start of the lines of latitude. In other words, the Equator is line zero.

To break things down further, the places on the Earth that are to the north of the Equator are known as the Northern Hemisphere. The places on the Earth that fall to the south of the Equator are in the area called the Southern Hemisphere. Hemisphere simply means half of a sphere.

Northern and Southern Hemispheres

Northern hemisphere

Southern hemisphere

From the imaginary grid that covers the Earth, there are eighty-nine lines that go north of the Equator and eighty-nine lines that run south. Each line forms a complete circle around the Earth. Because the Earth is thickest in the middle, the lines near the Equator are the longest.

The imaginary grid has eighty-nine lines that go north of the Equator and eighty-nine lines that run south

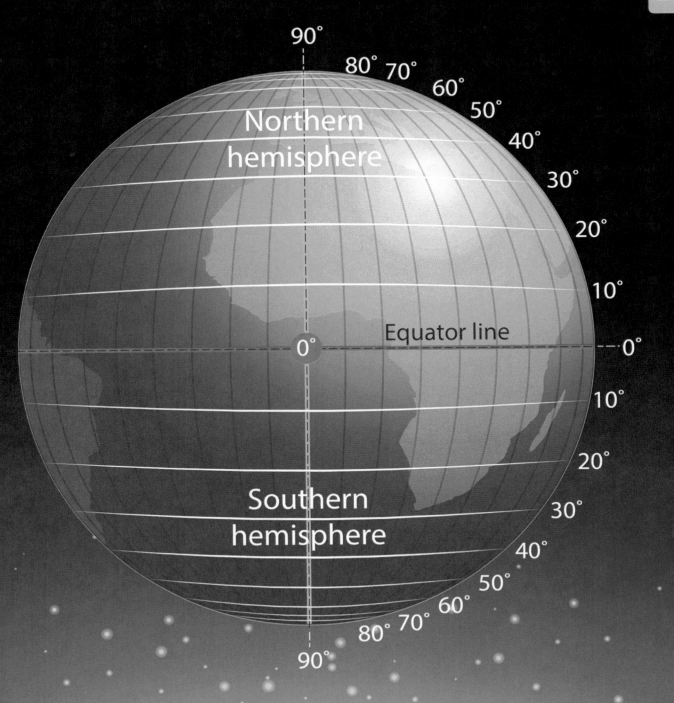

They gradually get shorter as they go towards the North Pole and the South Pole. Because the Earth is a sphere, each individual line of latitude goes around the Earth to form a complete circle.

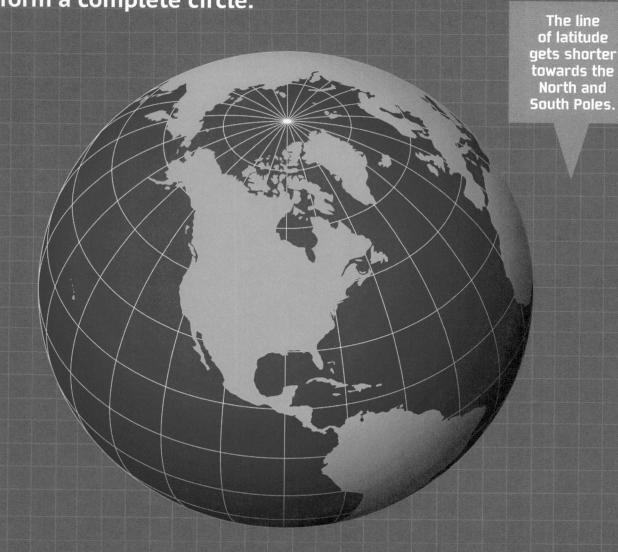

The line of latitude gets shorter towards the North and South Poles.

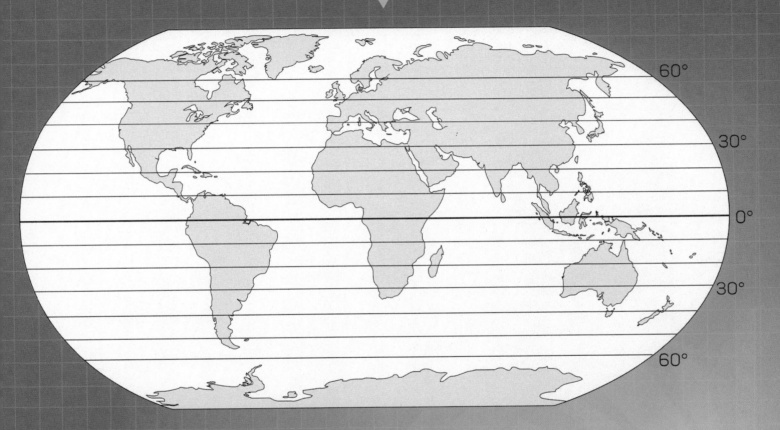

The lines of latitude show how far a place is from the Equator.

60°
30°
0°
30°
60°

Although the lines of latitude show an east to west direction on the Earth, they are used to show how far a position, or a place is from north to south of the Equator.

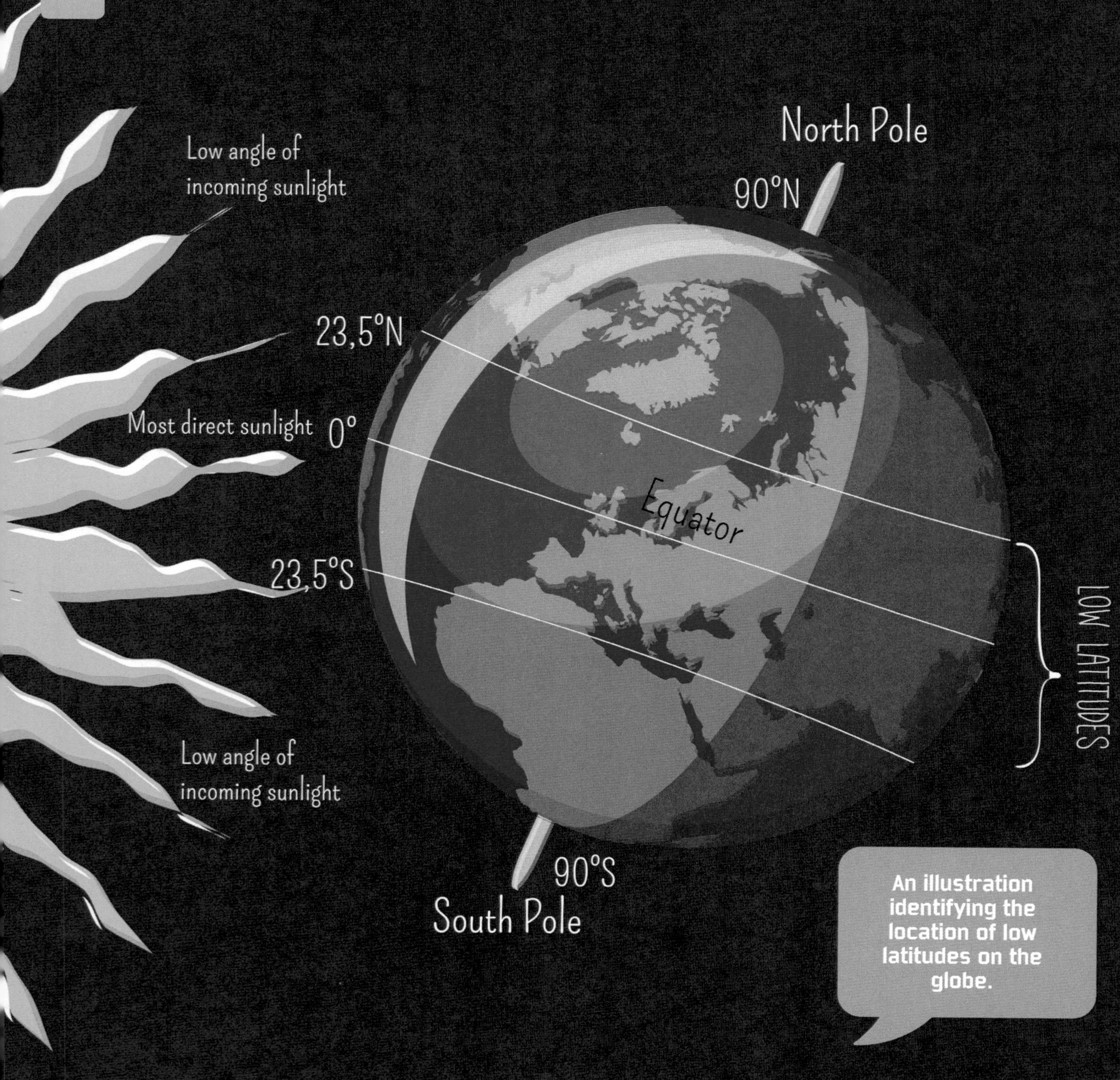

Low angle of
incoming sunlight

North Pole
90°N

23,5°N

Most direct sunlight   0°

Equator

23,5°S

LOW LATITUDES

Low angle of
incoming sunlight

90°S
South Pole

An illustration
identifying the
location of low
latitudes on the
globe.

There are also some special lines of latitude. They can help us guess what kind of land lie on certain areas of the Earth. The area of the Earth found between the two thirtieth parallels of latitude are called the low latitudes.

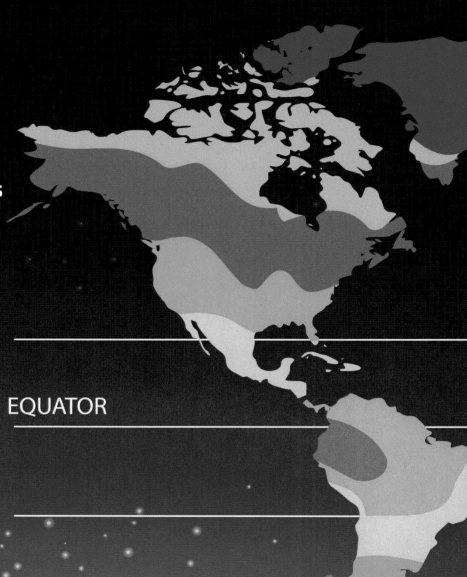

The lands and countries found in the low latitudes are usually very warm.

Low Latitudes

EQUATOR

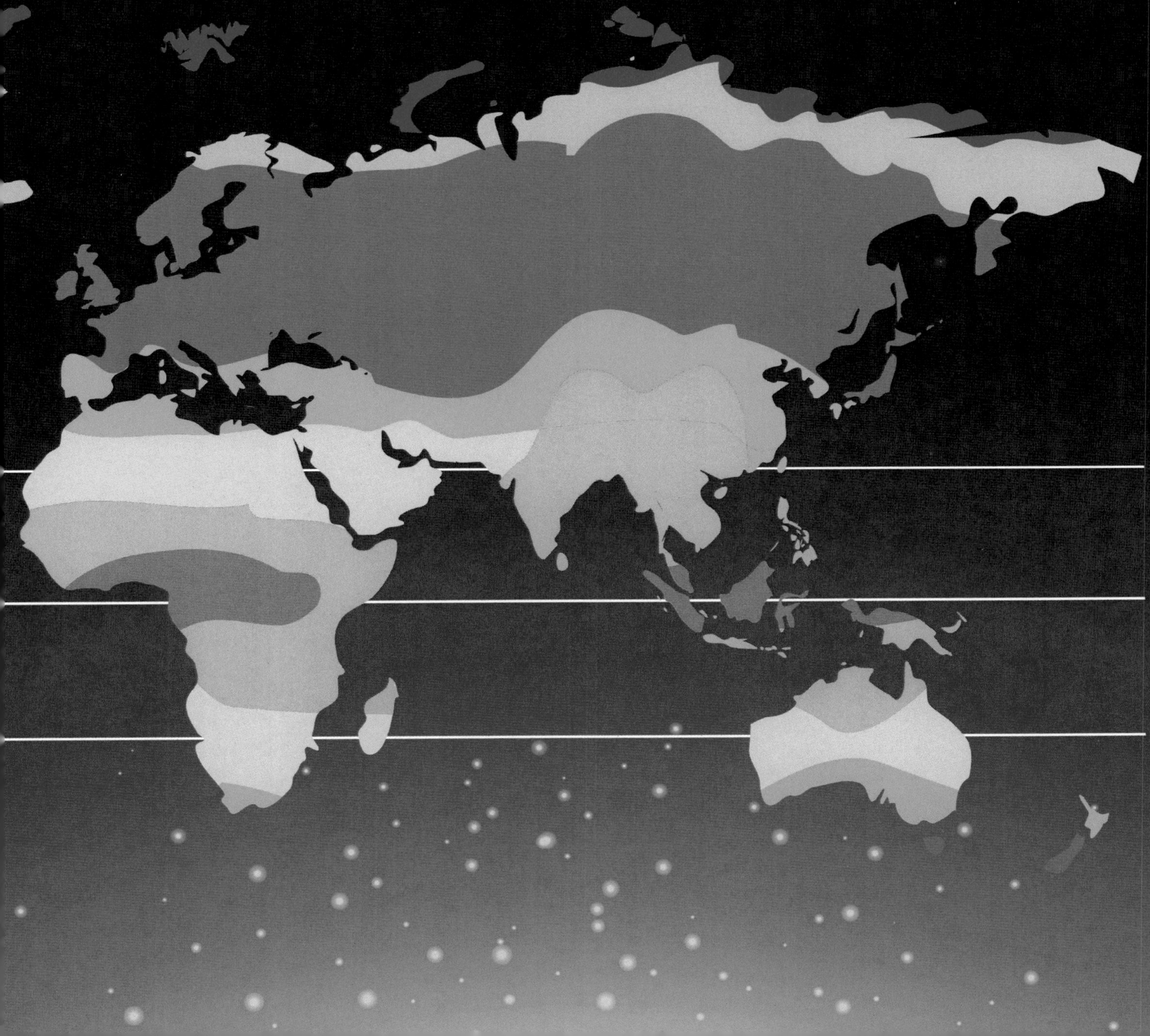

Low angle of
incoming sunlight

North Pole

66,5°N   90°N

HIGH LATITUDES

23,5°N

Most direct sunlight 0°

Equator

LOW LATITUDES

23,5°S

Low angle of
incoming sunlight

66,5°S

Antarctic Circle

HIGH LATITUDES

90°S

South Pole

The North and South
Poles are located on
high latitudes.

There are also areas of the Earth called the high latitudes. They are found to the north and the south of the sixtieth parallels of latitude. You can expect cold weather when you go to the higher latitudes.

Countries found in middle latitudes have four regular seasons

Low angle of incoming sunlight

North Pole

66,5°N

90°N

HIGH LATITUDES

23,5°N

MIDDLE LATITUDES

Most direct sunlight 0°

Equator

23,5°S

LOW LATITUDES

Low angle of incoming sunlight

66,5°S

Antarctic Circle

MIDDLE LATITUDES

90°S

HIGH LATITUDES

South Pole

The areas of the Earth that are in between these two regions are simply the middle latitudes. You would expect the temperatures in these areas to be less extreme with four regular seasons.

The reason the lines of latitude can help people guess what kind of temperatures to expect is because of the shape of the Earth and how it is tilted towards the sun. Since the Equator is the thickest part of the Earth, it is closer to the sun and receives more radiation or heat.

The lines of latitude help determine temperatures in certain regions of the Earth.

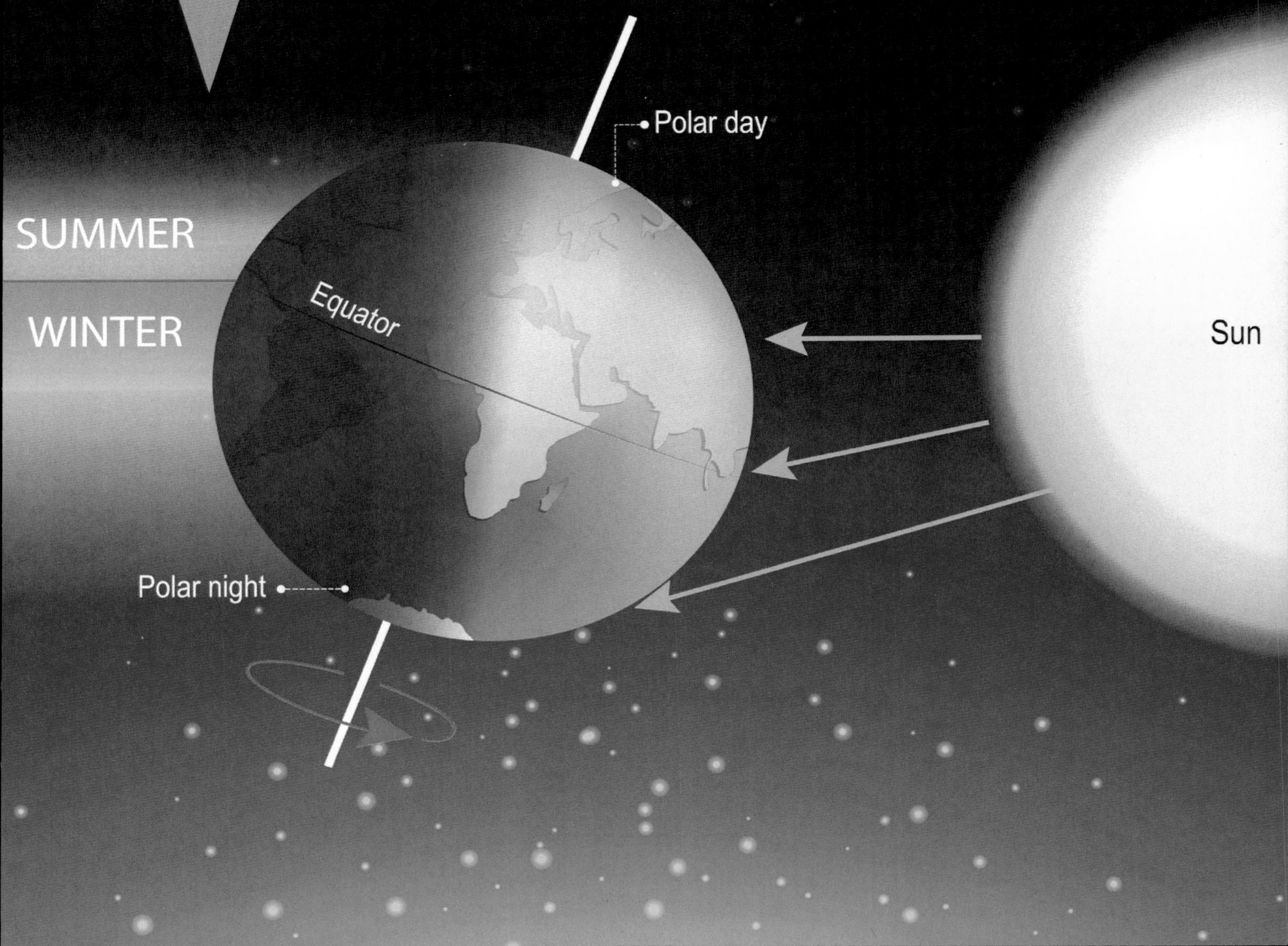

Polar day

SUMMER

WINTER

Equator

Sun

Polar night

Lines of latitude are measured in relation to the Equator. It is only natural that the further degrees north or south you get, the further away from the sun you would be, and the colder temperatures you would find.

Frozen sea, North Pole

In fact, at both the North and South poles, there is ice all year around.

Antarctica snow-capped mountains, South Pole

The tilt of the Earth on its axis as it orbits the sun also affects how we perceive the rising and setting of the suns.

Earth orbiting the sun

Perhaps you have noticed that there are longer days in summer and shorter days in winter. If you go far enough north or far enough south, you will find some season where the sun never sets or rises.

Summer night in Antarctica

You can determine when you have crossed a line on the Earth. The lines of the Arctic and Antarctic Circles represent the places where such a phenomenon will occur.

Arctic
Northern lights
in Norway

There are also the lines of the Tropic of Cancer and Capricorn. They represent the end of the zones where, at some point, the sun will be directly above. They straddle the Equator.

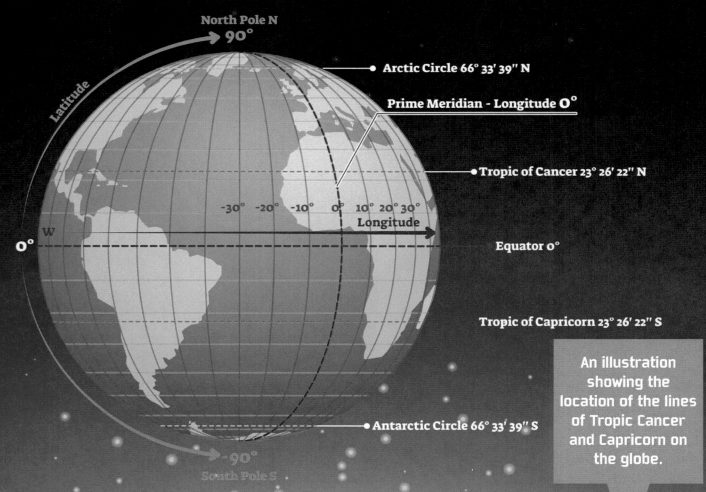

An illustration showing the location of the lines of Tropic Cancer and Capricorn on the globe.

LINES OF
LONGITUDE

Lines of longitude are the imaginary lines that go around the Earth in the opposite direction from the lines of latitude. In other words, they go from north to south. They are measured from both poles, the North Pole and the South Pole. They show where things are located on the Earth from east to west.

Longitude are lines that go from north to south

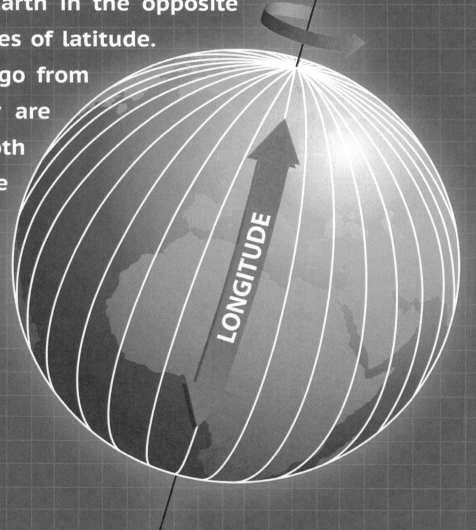

LONGITUDE

The starting point for the lines of longitude is called the Prime Meridian and it starts in Greenwich, England.

Prime Meridian, Greenwich where east meets west

The rest of the lines can also be called meridians or meridians of longitude. Much as the Equator is the starting point for the lines of latitude and is used to divide the Earth into the Northern Hemisphere and the Southern Hemisphere, the Prime Meridian also divides the Earth.

Longitude lines can also be called meridians

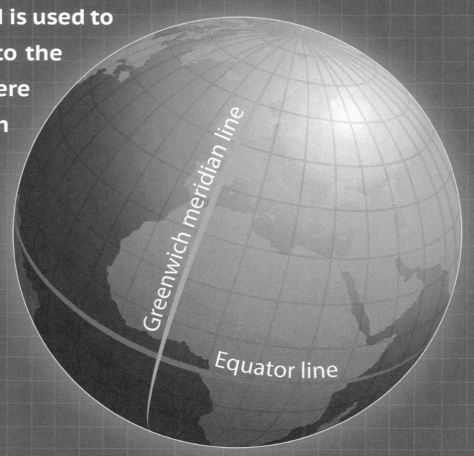

Greenwich meridian line

Equator line

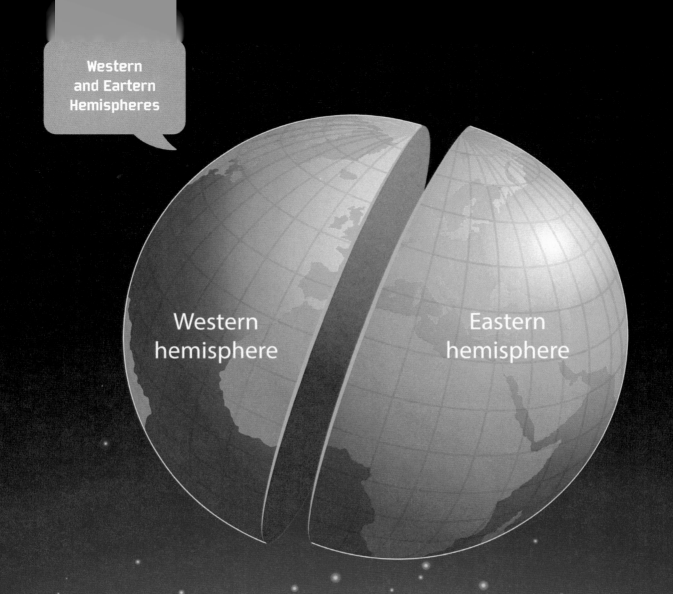

Western hemisphere

Eastern hemisphere

However, the meridians, or lines of longitude, divide the Earth into the Western Hemisphere and the Eastern Hemisphere.

There are one hundred and eighty lines that go from the west of the Prime Meridian and one hundred and eighty lines that go from the east of the Prime Meridian. All lines of longitude measure the same length and they come together at both poles.

There are a total of three hundred sixty lines that go from the west and east of the Prime Meridian.

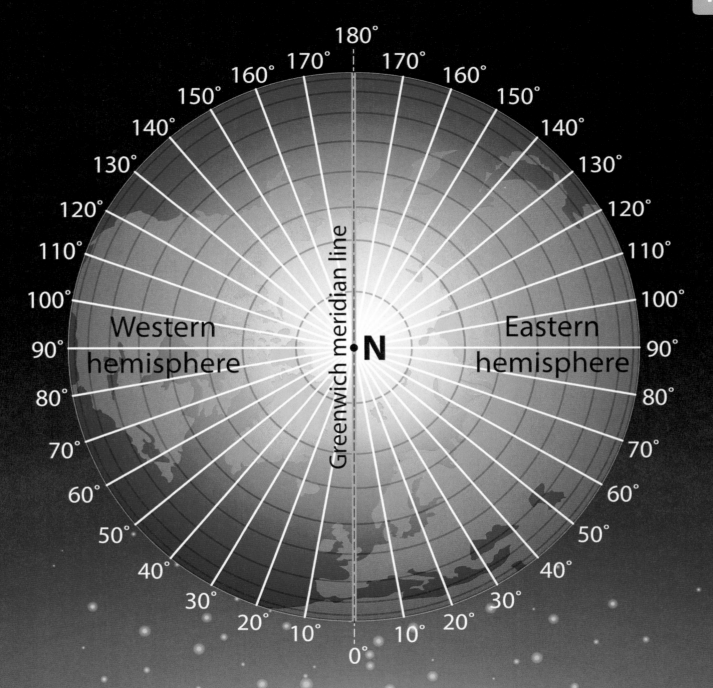

HOW THE LINES OF LATITUDE AND LONGITUDE PINPOINT PLACES ON THE EARTH

The imaginary lines of latitude and longitude make up a grid that covers the entire Earth. A location can be pinpointed by finding out which lines on the grid intersect at just the right spot.

A location can be pinpointed based on where the grids intersect.

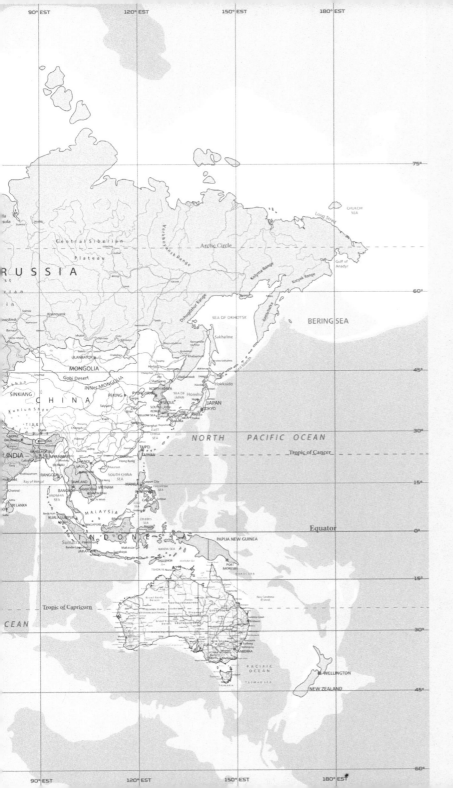

For example, the thirtieth line in the Northern Hemisphere intersects with the ninetieth line of the Western Hemisphere. The city of New Orleans can be found at that point of intersection.

The City of New Orleans is found in 30° Latitude, 90° west Longitude

Other cities like Cairo in Egypt also lie in the thirtieth line. There are also different cities like Port Arthur in Texas that are on the ninetieth line. Fortunately, neither of these cities lies on the same place where the lines crossover as New Orleans.

Cairo in Egypt also lies in the thirtieth line

The jargon used to describe these lines is degrees. Since the Earth is a sphere, all locations along any of the lines of longitude and latitude are the same distance from the center of the Earth. As a result, they will all have the same angle between the centre and the Equator. This is why we use the term degrees.

The term "degrees" is used to describe the lines of latitude and longitude.

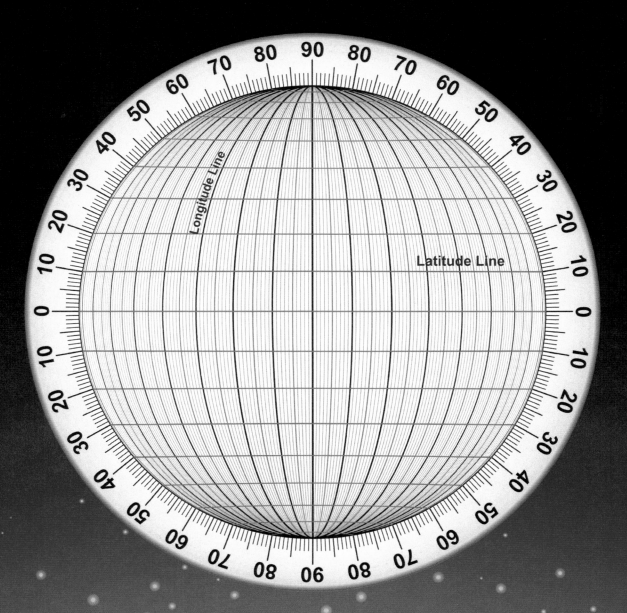

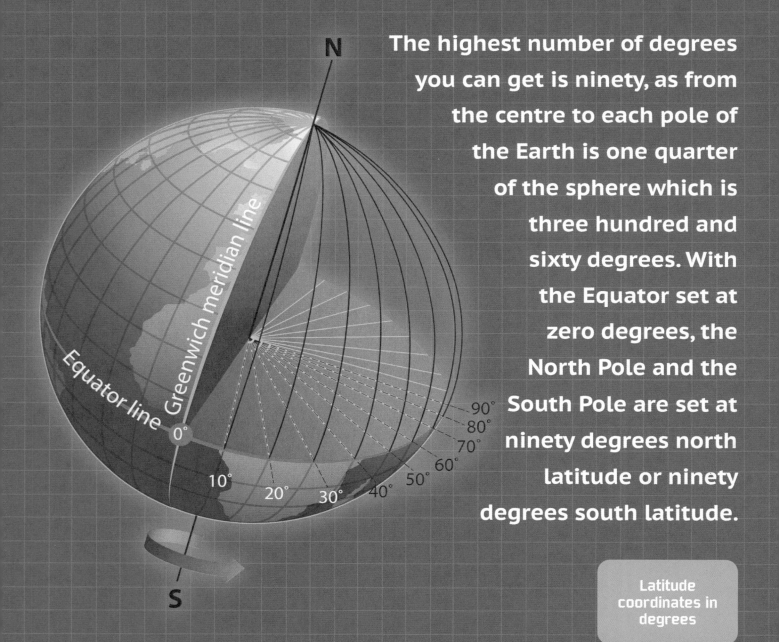

N

Greenwich meridian line

Equator line

0°

10°

20°

30°

40°

50°

60°

70°

80°

90°

S

The highest number of degrees you can get is ninety, as from the centre to each pole of the Earth is one quarter of the sphere which is three hundred and sixty degrees. With the Equator set at zero degrees, the North Pole and the South Pole are set at ninety degrees north latitude or ninety degrees south latitude.

Latitude coordinates in degrees

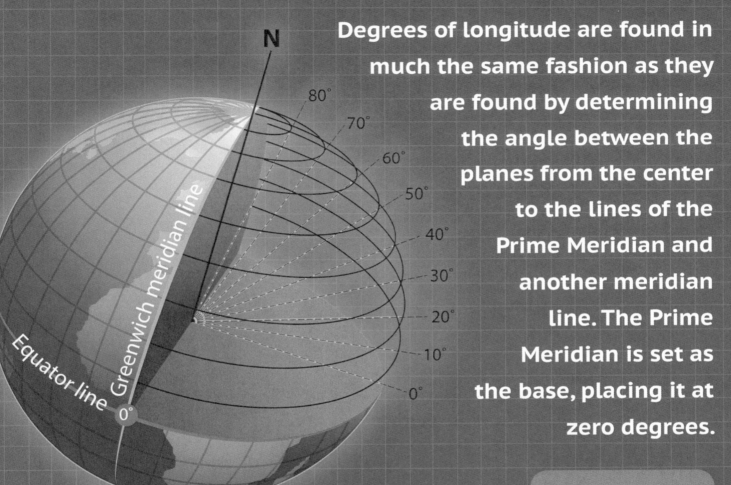

N

80°
70°
60°
50°
40°
30°
20°
10°
0°

Greenwich meridian line

Equator line

0°

S

Degrees of longitude are found in much the same fashion as they are found by determining the angle between the planes from the center to the lines of the Prime Meridian and another meridian line. The Prime Meridian is set as the base, placing it at zero degrees.

Degrees of longitude are found from the center to the lines of the Prime Meridian

Unlike with lines of latitude, lines of longitude go from zero to one hundred and eighty degrees. These degrees are counted towards the west or east. Since the Earth is a sphere with three hundred and sixty degrees, this means that one hundred and eighty degrees west is also the same as one hundred and eighty degrees east.

Lines of longitude go from zero to one hundred and eighty degrees

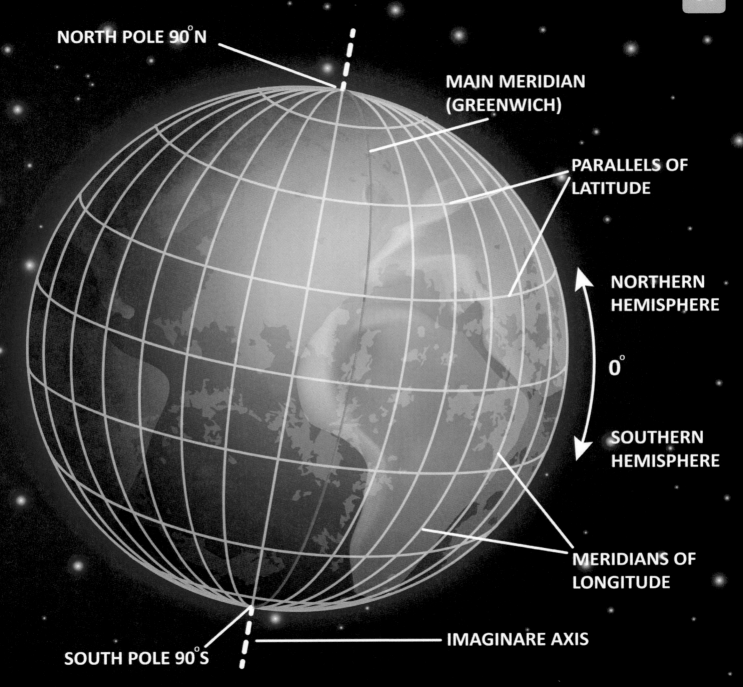

NORTH POLE 90°N

MAIN MERIDIAN (GREENWICH)

PARALLELS OF LATITUDE

NORTHERN HEMISPHERE

0°

SOUTHERN HEMISPHERE

MERIDIANS OF LONGITUDE

IMAGINARE AXIS

SOUTH POLE 90°S

I degree is equal to 60 minutes

$$1° = 60'$$

These degrees can be divided down further into what are called minutes, if more precision is needed. Minutes, true to the name, are broken down into sixtieths.

Now that you know all the jargon used, you can say that any location on Earth is located so many degrees and/or minutes of the Equator in either a northern or southern direction, and so many degrees and/or minutes of the Prime Meridian in an eastern or western direction.

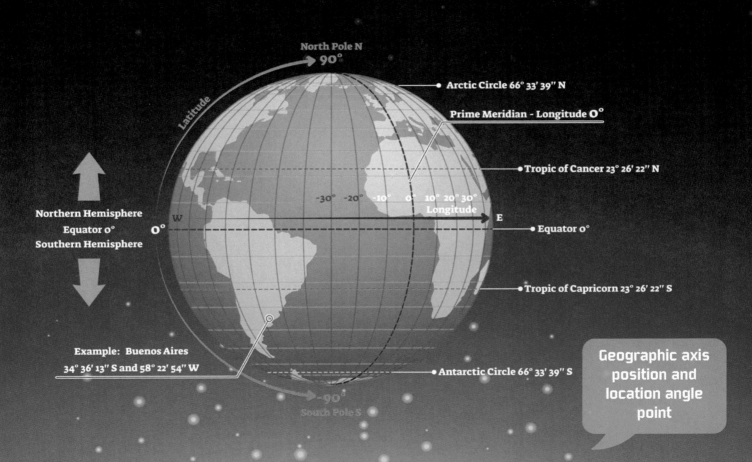

North Pole N
90°

Latitude

Arctic Circle 66° 33' 39" N

Prime Meridian - Longitude 0°

Tropic of Cancer 23° 26' 22" N

-30° -20° -10° 0° 10° 20° 30°
Longitude

E

Northern Hemisphere
Equator 0°
Southern Hemisphere

W

0°

Equator 0°

Tropic of Capricorn 23° 26' 22" S

Example: Buenos Aires
34° 36' 13" S and 58° 22' 54" W

Antarctic Circle 66° 33' 39" S

-90°
South Pole S

Geographic axis position and location angle point

ROME

6283 MI

LA HABANA

1632 MI

MEXICO

These measurements of location can even be turned into measurements in miles. This can be done because the lines are imaginary ones across the Earth and as a result have a pre-determined amount of distance between them.

Signs indicating the international capital distance in miles from Quito, Ecuador

JERUSALEN

7613 MI

As the Earth is around 25,000 miles around, if you divide that number by the total number of lines of latitude there are, three hundred and sixty, you will find each degree has approximately 69 miles. This is quite straightforward.

1° = 69 miles

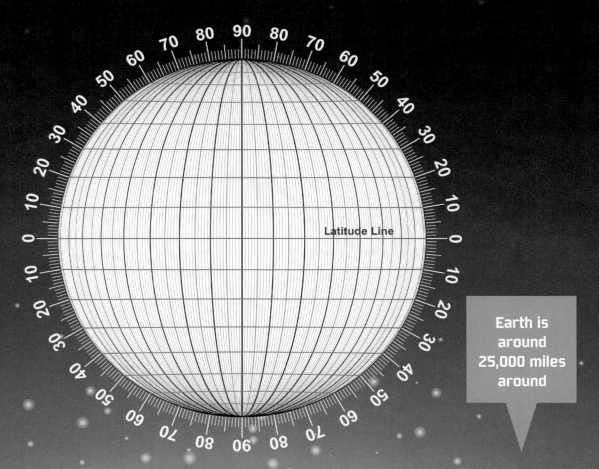

Latitude Line

Earth is around 25,000 miles around

The process of determining distance gets a little bit trickier when it comes to the degrees of longitude. It is trickier because the Earth is not actually a perfect sphere. It bulges more in the middle than it would if it were perfectly circular, and it is thinner up around the poles. The distance for degrees of longitude can vary from as much as 69 miles at the Equator to 0 at the two poles.

> Determining the distance of degrees of longitude is trickier because earth bulges in the middle and gets thinner up in the poles

As we can see, an accurate system of finding things on Earth has been put in place. By using the lines of latitude and longitude in the imaginary grid system that encircles the Earth, we can pinpoint any place with confidence.

Using latitude and longitude lines, we can easily locate any place

Measuring distance from one place to another

Visit

BABY PROFESSOR

EDUCATION KIDS

www.speedypublishing.com

to download Free Baby Professor eBooks
and view our catalog of new and exciting
Children's Books

Made in the USA
Monee, IL
18 February 2022

91431533R00045